THE MENTAL MAKEOVER

KICK YOUR 'BUTS' GOODBYE!

Don McArt

2 Minute Press
Boca Raton, Florida

The Mental Makeover: Kick Your 'Buts' Goodbye!

2 Minute Press Boca Raton, Florida

561.750.8095 info@thementalmakeover.com

Library of Congress Cataloging-in-Publication Data
McArt, Don

The Mental Makeover: Kick Your 'Buts' Goodbye!/ Don McArt.
1st ed.

ISBN 0-9722844-2-7
    1. self-help 2. inspiration 3. lifestyle

Edited by Deborah Lahr Lawlor

FIRST EDITION

This book is dedicated to all those looking for simple answers to complex problems and willing to scientifically use their creative power in finding them.

The author wishes to express his appreciation to Debbi and John Lawlor for their invaluable, supportive and dedicated hard work in making this book possible.

"What lies behind us and what lies before us are tiny matters compared to what lies within us."

Ralph Waldo Emerson

Contents

Don't miss this page!

Millions of people today are leading lives of unhappiness, frustration or misery, little realizing that they have the power within themselves to change those conditions!

Instead, they believe that their situation, their lot in life, is one dictated by some external factors and, when told otherwise, quickly become one of the, "Yes, but…" brigade, defensively telling us *why* they can't do it. "Yes, but I'm too old." – "Yes, but I'm too fat, or too thin, too short or too tall." – "Yes, but I don't have enough money – or enough education – or any opportunities – or the right connections," etc. etc.

These are the "yes, but" people – those who stay confined in their own self-imposed mental prisons, completely unaware that if they would only *get off their "buts,"* they could freely walk out of those prisons and begin the first steps towards making significant, positive and productive changes in their lives!

History is loaded with successful examples of those who gave up their beliefs in limitation and replaced them with the awareness that within us all is a *creative power* that responds to the nature of our beliefs, whatever they are. They learned to rely on it for overcoming the obstacles in their path and achieving the fulfillment of their dreams and goals.

YOU can be one of them, but, as always, the choice is yours…and so is the responsibility!

The Mental Makeover:

Here are 52 ways to improve your days – 52 proven ways to help overcome negative, limiting, self-defeating thinking and provide the necessary tools for a successful Mental Makeover.

Each will take less than two minutes to read, but can help make substantial, constructive changes in all aspects of your life – as they have in mine!

Don McArt
Boca Raton, Florida
April, 2004

I CHOOSE TO PRODUCE RESULTS THAT I WANT!

…but they never pan out.

Why do some accomplish their goals, and others don't? How is it that some are able to turn their dreams into realities, and others can't?

The answer is one word: *choice*. Actually, everyone could if they only realized it.

The same creative power is in us all. It is a *power without limits*, which is *always* ready to act on our convictions, no matter what they may be. *Believe you can, and you will. Believe you can't, and you won't.*

The person with a dream and a conviction is the one who has the ingredients for eventual success. The person without conviction remains little more than just another disappointed dreamer.

The irony of it, though, is no matter what the results, the *same* power produces them all. The only difference is the *belief* behind them. It obeys all orders *convincingly* given, whether to our advantage or detriment. Its only duty is to produce, and produce it does…whether it's our fondest dream or worst fear. Use your power wisely and produce the results you desire!

I CHOOSE TO BELIEVE IN A CREATIVE POWER!

…but how do I beef up my belief?

The ability and willingness to commit to a belief, 100%, is a combination that can work wonders in the life of anyone.

The reluctance, or refusal, to do so is a sure sign of trouble up ahead, because the two, belief and commitment, go hand in hand.

Belief, without commitment, is only half of the formula for success at any time in any life. Commitment without belief is like a cart without a horse. It's not going anywhere because nothing is pulling it. The willingness to commit with every fiber of your being is required at any time.

It becomes even easier when you know you're dealing with a creative power, which *must respond according to the nature of your belief.*

This removes the guesswork from the entire operation. It is no longer a question of "Will it?" or "Won't it?" All doubt is eliminated from your mind when you *know* the source of your strength and accept its *unlimited* capacity for achievement.

Commitment, then, should be a totally *logical* action.

I CHOOSE TRUST RATHER THAN FEAR!

…but I can never have the kind of life I really want.

The creative power within us all is capable of fulfilling our fondest dreams or materializing our greatest fears. And, as hard as it is to imagine at times, we *each* decide exactly which it will be.

Life asks us, "What do you want?" And we answer with the various beliefs that *dominate* our thinking, whether we realize it or not.

For those able to completely trust this creative power within themselves, there is no challenge too great to overcome, no goal beyond conquest.

Every accomplishment for greater good, down through the ages, has come about by the positive, constructive use of this one creative principle. So, too, has the misery and suffering — by negatively using this inner power.

Its obligation is to respond to the *nature* of our beliefs. *Our* obligation is to be so selective that our beliefs reflect *only* the elements that will produce the highest good in every aspect of our lives.

The good life is ours for the thinking! It is never necessary to doubt or fear *if* we know we are in control and using a power that is *without limitation.*

I CHOOSE TO LIVE LIFE BOLDLY!

…but won't people think I'm cocky?

Those who believe there is an always-available, unlimited, creative power within themselves can have a profoundly positive effect on the way they live their lives…how they deal with their experiences…how they treat other people…how they treat themselves, if they so choose.

People who know that life is *for* them, and that they are always playing with four aces, *can afford to be bold…can afford to be courageous…can afford to venture forth into uncharted waters!*

Those who are constantly in touch with the *true source* of their strength *can afford to dream their dreams…tackle the tough challenges…turn the other cheek!*

People who know they are only limited by their beliefs *can get answers…can afford to be gracious…can afford to feel confident…can afford to be enthusiastic!*

Those who know they were created to succeed *can be supportive…can be non-judgmental…can risk disapproval by others!*

This creative power is yours for the believing. It will be as consistent in providing positive results for you, as *you* are consistent in making positive use of it!

I CHOOSE CONSISTENT BELIEF!

…but I do believe and nothing seems to change.

Those of us who profess to be positive thinkers can discover how positive we actually are by running a periodic check on our attitudes. Much like the oil level in an automobile crankcase tells us the amount of oil in it, our *attitudes* will tell us just how much *actual positive belief* there is in our thinking. *Our attitudes reflect our belief in the creative power within and our capacity to fully use it.*

The power is activated *solely* on the basis of the sum total of our beliefs. If our belief is weak or vacillating, our results will be likewise, no matter what kind of a thinker we may call ourselves.

The bottom line is *total belief*. We either have it, or we don't. *Total belief*, held to *consistently*, will produce results of a corresponding nature. There is no other way it can be.

Great good in our lives will never come from limited, fearful, doubtful or wishful thinking. Nor will it come from skepticism.

Our vision must be *clear* and *consistent*, no matter what is going on around us. It's only the person who's able to see *beyond* what things are at the moment to what things *can be* that truly deserves to be called a positive thinker.

I CHOOSE MY OWN EXPRESSION OF SUCCESS!

…but nobody's ever been able to do it.

Simply because another person has failed at something doesn't mean that *you* will, too. On the other hand, it just might.

The truth is that we are each a unique, individualized point of consciousness, able to determine the nature of our experiences by the nature of our beliefs.

If my limited belief has produced limited results for me, it merely indicates the quality of *my* belief at that particular moment in my life. To identify your experience with my *potential* for accomplishment is senseless, since *we are each free to set that limit for ourselves*. My results and your results could vary diametrically, depending on the differences in our respective beliefs. What might have been a minor disaster for me could be a great success for you.

Our beliefs are our most important assets, for they shape our reality.

Thus, the worst mistake that any of us could make would be to accept somebody else's limited beliefs as our own. To do so would automatically mean putting a cap on that which could conceivably bring us an entirely different result.

Make the most of whom you are. *Refuse to accept needless limitations about yourself*!

I CHOOSE TO KNOW THAT I AM A UNIQUE, WORTHWHILE HUMAN BEING!

…but I feel others are so much better than I am.

Self-image. Is it important? You bet it is!

There is nothing more important than the way we see ourselves because this view will have a direct bearing on everything about us: our health, happiness, work, income and relationships with others.

A high *self-regard* is essential for enjoying life fully. Without a healthy sense of our own worth, we automatically consign ourselves to living life at a level far below our true potential.

Why do so many of us think of ourselves as a bargain basement item rather than something of great value? Why is it that we so often settle for less, less than the best that we are or could be?

The answer is that we have simply *misidentified ourselves.* We have failed to recognize the truth that *we are each created as a totally unique, worthwhile human being.*

To make the most of this great gift, however, it takes *our recognition* of it. It takes a determination to stop comparing ourselves to others and, instead, dedicate ourselves to bringing forth all that we have each been given to the very best of our ability. *It can be done and you can do it*!

I CHOOSE SELF-ACCEPTANCE!

…but I don't really like who I am.

As children, one of the most enjoyable sensations we can experience is to feel that others are proud of us. When we are adults, this continues to be a very stimulating tonic, as we often go to great lengths to win the approval of others.

It is a mark of maturity, however, when we finally realize that, pleasing as the applause of others may be, it is mild in comparison to the rewards that come from being pleased with ourselves.

This is the *ultimate*, because if we are not proud of ourselves, the acceptance by others will do little to relieve the pain of self-loathing we may feel.

Self-acceptance and self-love are essential for living a well-balanced, fulfilling life! There is no other way it can be done. Without them, the creative part of our mind, *that element which produces the conditions in our lives according to the nature of our beliefs*, is working from a pattern that can only turn out results that reflect our feelings of rejection and unworthiness.

How does one cultivate feelings of self-acceptance and self-love? *By working at it.* By doing the kinds of things that make you feel good about yourself. By treating others the way *you* like to be treated…with forgiveness, consideration, thoughtfulness, compassion, respect, acceptance and love.

By fully accepting your own special uniqueness and then conducting yourself with integrity at all times and, by doing your best with every opportunity you have, you'll soon find there's nothing to hate yourself for or to feel unworthy about.

I CHOOSE TO BE ENTHUSIASTIC!

…but I don't want to look childish.

If you don't have *enthusiasm* in your life, *you need it*! What's more, you can have it.

Enthusiasm is not something you're either born with or without. Everybody has a capacity for enthusiasm, although, admittedly, it must be cultivated.

Enthusiasm is best nourished and developed in a positive, appreciative environment. Enthusiastic and positive people will always go far toward reaching whatever goals they may set for themselves.

With enthusiasm, we have a light in the occasional dark tunnels of life. We have the spark that keeps our dreams alive, our courage strong, our beliefs consistent.

Give a child the gift of enthusiasm, and you have given him or her one of life's greatest assets.

Teach the child that there is never a need to be anything but enthusiastic and confidently expectant towards life, and you have gone a long way towards giving that young person the necessary tools to triumphantly deal with any crisis and endure any conflict.

An old dog *can* learn new tricks. If your enthusiasm has lost its vitality, do everything possible to revive it. Don't let the young dogs have all the fun!

I CHOOSE TO PERSEVERE!

…but I really don't see how it can happen.

How many of our great dreams wither and die on the vines of our minds simply because we have become discouraged, lost hope and given up? Far too many, unfortunately.

Although we had the desire to see our dreams become realities, we didn't give them the *proper nourishment*. To give our dreams the *proper nourishment* means we must do two important things:

First, we must become *convinced* that our goal or something even better can be accomplished. Just *wishing* or *hoping* is not enough. We must *know* that somehow, and in some way, it *can* be done…that there is nothing impossible to the creative mind within!

Second, we must be determined that it *will* be done, and that we will *persevere* until we see the results we want.

The decision should be one that leaves no room for doubt…one capable of carrying us through to eventual success *if* our determination is sustained.

Abraham Lincoln once said, "Determine that the thing can and shall be done, and then we shall find the way. The horse must go before the cart." And so it is in dealing with our dreams. We must do the *mental preparation* before going forth in a flurry of activity.

Once we have made this all-out commitment in complete faith and trust, then is the time to take whatever initial action seems appropriate, *knowing* that we are on the path to ultimate victory.

I CHOOSE POSITIVE HABITS!

…but bad habits are so hard to change.

Habits, we've all got them. In fact, there isn't much we do that isn't a habit of some kind.

Many habits are helpful, enabling us to do things with comfort and ease. Others, however, block us from the good things in life we could be having. Unfortunately, we often stay locked into these negative habits, feeling that there isn't too much we can do about them, that this is "just the way we are." But, it's simply not so.

While it's true that we are creatures of habit, it's also true that we, ourselves, created those habits – the good ones as well as the bad ones.

Lack of confidence, for example, is nothing more than habitually thinking of ourselves in a pessimistic or defeatist way. These are the habits that rob us of our vitality, creativity and self-expression. That's the bad news. The good news is that we also have the ability to make *new choices* and form *new habits* if we really want to.

It all starts with making the *decision*, the decision to change from this to that, and deciding to give our new goal the same amount of energy that we used in creating the old.

Secondly, it takes *discipline*. There must be no wavering back and forth…wondering whether we made the right choice, or whether we'll actually succeed.

The final step is *determination*…knowing that whatever we can conceive of, *we can achieve* by properly using the creative power within.

I CHOOSE TO DREAM!

…but none of my dreams ever work out.

One of the unfortunate things about growing up is that too often we stop dreaming – not the nighttime variety but the daytime kind.

We tend to forget that the automobile, the airplane, radio and television, for example, were each nothing more than somebody's daydream long before they became tangible realities for the world to enjoy. They were daydreams that someone *believed* in.

We've all had our dreams somewhere along the line, but many of us have simply given up on the possibility of ever achieving them. We've thrown in the towel because we didn't realize that the daydream, itself, can be an inner urging to express ourselves in a particular way. We didn't believe the way would be provided for us to fulfill those dreams if we persistently and confidently pushed forward.

The fact is that *every dream is the seed of a potential creation, and each mind is a fertile garden for growing that seed.*

Put *new* life in *your* life – no matter where you are on the age scale – by picking out a dream you believe in and living as though you *expect* it to happen. You won't be disappointed!

I CHOOSE WITH INSIGHT AND DISCIPLINE!

…but I just had to have it.

Did you ever buy something in the heat of excitement and later regret that you'd spent more than you'd intended? If so, consider yourself in good company because most of us have done the same thing at one time or another.

The intensity of our desire and the impulse of the moment can sometimes make us oblivious to the price tag on the item we covet, and it can come as a painful shock, later, when we realize the full amount of our financial obligation.

The price tag was there all the time, of course, but the anticipated pleasure of our purchase was so great that it just didn't clearly register.

It's interesting, though, how our pleasure is often considerably diminished when we are subsequently confronted with the unpleasant consequences of our rashness.

Life is full of things with price tags on them, actually, and they aren't all found in just the places where we shop. Every choice we make has a price tag, a payoff, somewhere down the line. Often, for the same reasons, we frequently ignore those price tags, until we are rudely confronted with the results our choices have caused.

To avoid aftershock of one kind or another, think twice before you decide and then, with insight and discipline, decide whether you're willing to pay that price.

I CHOOSE THE PROPER PRIORITIES!

...but I just have too much to do and too little time.

We each have the same amount of time at our disposal every day. No favoritism there.

The question is: *How* do we use it? Do we have a clear picture of what it is we want to accomplish during that time? Are we able to say "no" to what might keep us from achieving our goal and "yes" to the proper priorities?

Too often those of us who desire more out of life go about trying to get these things in a very haphazard, undisciplined way. Too often our *results* are also fragmented. *Those who cannot successfully manage their time soon become victims of their own frustrations.*

People with a purpose, with a desire, a goal, or a dream need to use their time carefully and wisely, allowing *nothing* to enter into their thinking that would make them doubt their ability to achieve. Accordingly, nothing should be allowed to divert or dissipate their creative energy.

Time is valuable! Clear thought is valuable. Use them both wisely and achieve the results you deserve!

I CHOOSE TO MAKE A DECISION AND GO FOR IT!

…but I'm afraid to commit in case it's wrong.

A push...that's exactly what many of us seem to be waiting for...someone to come along and give us a push in the right direction. Those who do this find that it can result in a lifetime of frustration, never realizing that it is we ourselves who must do whatever pushing is to be done. Only *we* can effectively give ourselves the go-ahead sign.

In other words, those waiting for someone else to help light their fuse and ignite the spark of energy and enthusiasm necessary for successful accomplishments are in for a long wait, because that's not the way life works. *The only push that will ever be of any significant value to any of us is the one we give ourselves.*

The hardest thing for many of us to do is make a *decision.* Thus, the first step to becoming a successful self-pusher is to decide what we want to accomplish and then set that choice up as a specific goal for ourselves. A *clear vision* of the thing we desire is essential. After all, if *we* don't know, who else does? Remember, we are dealing with a creative power that can do *anything* for us, but it acts only on the instructions that *we* convincingly give it with our beliefs.

The push in life with the successful payoff will be the one we give ourselves by making that firm decision to start, then going for it – no holds barred!

I CHOOSE
TO RISE
ABOVE
MY DIFFICULTIES!

…but my life today is keeping me stuck.

Ready for a new start? Why not? Why not turn from the disappointments, heartaches and failures of the past to creating something better for yourself?

It can be done. There is nothing that holds any of us permanently locked into any one state of mind and, of course, that is where all change must start – *in our thinking*.

What an exciting challenge it can be to successfully move from one state of being to another! To rise triumphantly over the difficulties and obstacles of the past as we systematically replace the thoughts of doubt and fear with those of faith and confidence.

Let's face it, feeling sorry for ourselves is easy, probably one of the easiest things we can do. It takes practically no effort, and would be great if it helped. But it doesn't. There is nothing positive that comes from self-pity.

On the other hand, if you channel that thought energy into a *revitalized* belief about yourself, coupled with an awakened awareness that by changing your thinking, you can actually change the nature of events and conditions in your life, then you've taken the first important, productive step to climbing up out of whatever your personal pit may be and moving on towards better things ahead, no matter what your age!

I CHOOSE TO MANAGE MY THOUGHTS!

…but I am in the midst of a real crisis.

A crisis is something most of us have faced at one period or another and may be even facing right now. There is no time in life that is more important!

A crisis is important because, no matter what conditions may have brought us to this point, we *always* have the ability to decide *how* we are going to handle it.

It depends on whether we give in to the frequent panic, depression or apparent hopelessness of the moment and mentally throw in the towel, or know that, in spite of whatever the crisis may be, *we* hold the trump card. While we may be physically, emotionally or financially challenged in one way or another, *there need never be any such limitation on our thoughts*, and in our *thoughts* is where the *solution* to any crisis must begin.

It is through our *thoughts* that we become either open or closed to an inflow of fresh ideas, new opportunities and changed conditions. It is by our *thoughts* that we can actually take control of a crisis and give it an entirely different label.

Make no mistake about it. *There is an inner creative power that responds to the nature of our thinking.* Face each crisis courageously. Use that great gift confidently. Become the master of your own destiny!

I CHOOSE TO CHANGE MY THINKING!

...but my past record is against me.

One of the greatest privileges we each have is being able to start over.

That doesn't mean we all take advantage of it, by any means, but we each have the opportunity to do so anytime we choose.

No matter what our experiences have been in the past, no matter how frustrating, humiliating or disappointing, we have the ability to reformulate them – to create an entirely *different* set of circumstances for ourselves.

The important thing to remember is that new experiences start with a *change* in our thinking. This simply means that, no matter what the conditions of the moment may be, no matter how remote the possibility of improvement might appear, no matter how locked in to whatever our present state we seem to be, by simply *changing the nature of our thinking*, we can take the first important step toward making a new start – if we really want to. And that's the good news.

The bad news is that many people let their past experiences cripple them mentally. Rather than rebuilding on whatever is to be learned and making a new start, they remain fearful that the future will hold only additional turmoil and failure.

The fact is that *our future will hold exactly what we are able to believe* it will, and we can start from right where we are!

I CHOOSE TO BELIEVE THAT I AM SUPERIOR TO ANY PROBLEM!

...but this problem is different.

Problems? We all have them. They're a part of living. How we *handle* our problems, however, is something else – something that can either make us or break us.

Some will consistently come up smelling like a rose no matter what difficulties they encounter. Others will be hard-pressed to keep from being plowed under by the slightest force.

There is nothing we will ever learn that is more important than the fact that we are each *superio*r to any problem we will ever face – *superior* in the sense that we have within ourselves the ability to successfully handle whatever the problem may be.

Human progress, down through the ages, has come from people solving their problems. These were people who refused to be intimidated by their challenge of the moment and, instead, approached it as an opportunity, convinced they somehow would emerge triumphantly from the experience, no matter what, with greater understanding and wisdom. These were the ones who had the courage to look away from the problem to the ultimate, universal source of all knowledge and power – *trusting completely* that whatever answer was needed would ultimately be provided!

I CHOOSE TO REPROGRAM MYSELF!

...but I couldn't possibly have programmed all that other stuff.

An airplane set on automatic pilot will head straight for the place it is programmed for.

Human beings, programmed in a particular way, will do the same thing. If they're looking for trouble, they'll find it. If expecting difficulties, they'll have them. Our thought atmosphere attracts the conditions in our lives just as surely as the automatic pilot in an airplane guides it in whatever direction it's set.

Life reacts to us as we feel and believe. This merely means we attract to ourselves according to the beliefs held in our subconscious minds.

To find out how you are programmed, look at the conditions in your life right now, since they will accurately give you a reading of what's going on inside your personal control panel.

If you are dissatisfied, why not *reprogram* yourself? In the long run, it's far more rewarding than running away or withdrawing from life. And, it's not hard to do. Begin by building a new thought atmosphere, a new series of beliefs just as you would change the direction of the automatic pilot if you wanted to fly towards New York rather than Mexico City. The automatic pilot can be set to take you in either direction. Likewise, your thought atmosphere will produce *whatever* you program it for.

If you want to go to New York, set your course for New York and nowhere else. If you desire specific results, focus your thinking on *that* – and nothing less!

I CHOOSE TO REACH MY GOAL WITH RENEWED ENERGY!

…but I'm really frustrated.

Frustration is something we all feel at times.

The question is: What *kind* of frustration does it amount to? Is it the kind that only makes us dig deeper for the answers that have so far eluded us, convinced that somehow, someway we'll find them? Or is it the kind that turns into a feeling of hopelessness about ever reaching our objective?

The interesting thing is that the same set of conditions can produce either kind of frustration, depending on the individual. Just as one person will see nothing but opportunities in nearly everything, and someone else will see only dead ends, so it is with the various frustrations in our lives. They can either propel us forward toward a goal, or make us drop the quest completely.

Those who clearly understand that, if properly used, their creative power will always bring them the results they desire, are the ones who overcome frustration and use a temporary setback as simply a time to reassess their position and set out toward their goals with renewed energy.

Proper use, of course, includes the maintenance of a positive, open and expectant attitude, no matter what the conditions may be at any given moment, and a willingness to actively investigate all opportunities.

Use your frustration wisely. Let it work *for* you, not *against* you!

I CHOOSE PATIENCE WITH CONFIDENCE!

...but I get scared I'm not doing enough.

For those wanting to make changes in their lives, patience is crucial.

Patience, unfortunately, is something far too few of us really understand, usually regarding it as something we try after all else has failed.

This is mistaken reasoning. Patience is never a matter of resignedly folding our hands and sitting back, hoping things will somehow work out. It is the furthest thing from being passive or an excuse for doing nothing.

True patience, instead, is a *dynamic mental activity*...a vital part of the whole changing process. It is confidently used by those who know they always have the capability of changing the conditions in their lives by changing their thinking.

Those who understand the power of their thought will face any goal calmly and confidently, knowing the control is within themselves. They will also recognize the importance of *patiently* maintaining that confidence at its *highest level* so as to allow their creative power to bring forth the desired results.

Thought is the starting point in the creative chain and, when coupled with belief, there is *no limit* to its possibilities if properly sustained. Patience should be used with unconditional expectancy!

I CHOOSE TO LOSE THE INERTIA HABIT!

...but I just can't seem to get going.

There probably aren't many of us who haven't gone through periods in our lives when we just didn't feel like doing anything. Some may be in such a period right now.

It's technically called *inertia*, and it can frequently come after we have experienced a major disappointment, loss, defeat or rejection. It doesn't happen overnight, as a general rule, but develops over a period of time, and eventually we get the feeling of, "What's the use?" We may have made a mistake along the way, for example, and the fear of doing it again practically immobilizes us to the point that we won't risk taking another chance.

Inertia, once it has become a habit, can be insidious, not only holding us back from doing what we have been doing, but also from initiating anything new for ourselves. We become passive and tired. Like a bump on a log, we just exist. Nothing seems to matter. Inertia has drained us of our energy and keeps us in a state of fatigue. We have surrendered to fear!

The cure is to recognize inertia as an acquired habit pattern and, as such, know it can be traded for another, more productive pattern. Refuse to continue in a mentally fatigued state for one minute longer. Know that you are only defeated if you *think* you are defeated and that *you can turn anything that happens to you into a profitable experience if you really want to.* Acknowledge the creative power within yourself - and *use it*!

I CHOOSE ENTHUSIASM, NO MATTER WHAT!

…but, let's face it, I've run out of steam.

Most of us would probably like to think we are young-at-heart, no matter how far along the road we are chronologically. But is it necessarily true?

Have we, for instance, been able to maintain our youthful enthusiasm for living and optimism for the future no matter how many hard knocks we've experienced? Or have we let them make us cold, callous, cynical and bitter?

Have we weathered our personal stormy weather, still honestly believing in the fundamental goodness of mankind?

Have we developed the ability to continually invest new vitality into old relationships and be ever on the lookout for new opportunities in our work?

Have we discovered that our state of mind has a direct bearing on our state of health and everything else we experience?

Have we become convinced that no matter what the problem, there is *always* a solution and that we will find it?

Have we realized the necessity for being helpful, encouraging, supportive and loving in our dealings with others and regarding their successes as equally as important as our own?

These are the qualities of the young-at-heart. You be the judge.

I CHOOSE TO BANISH WORRY!

…but I'm afraid things won't work out.

There is little that can destroy our enjoyment of life more than worry. There is nothing that represents a greater waste of time and energy than worry.

Worry is an art form for many people.

It is a *misuse* of our creative power. It is *negative anticipation* – the "art" of actually experiencing an unpleasant event without it necessarily ever happening.

Worry is a habit, a *destructive* habit. It represents *misplaced faith*. Worry is senseless for anyone who understands the principles of how his or her mind works.

If you believe that life is fundamentally good and nothing can happen to you without your giving consent to it – at some level of your thinking – then it becomes a matter of putting your energy where your belief is and calmly sitting back in perfect trust, free from the destructive tension and stress that worry can produce.

Instead of worrying about the challenges in life, face them squarely, head on, with the conviction that you are aligned with a universal presence which will guide you into your true place and highest good – as you *expect* it and *accept* it.

Always use proper caution, yes, but waste your life worrying, and it's your own fault!

I CHOOSE TO LABEL EVERYTHING GOOD!

…but not everything is good.

An attitude of gratitude always pays dividends for the person able to genuinely maintain it.

Unfortunately, it's not that easy to do, particularly when the world appears to have turned against us and nothing is going well, or when the bottom has apparently dropped out of our fondest dreams, and we find ourselves facing one dead end after another. Suddenly it seems there's nothing to be grateful for.

Given the right conditions, we all find ourselves occasionally slipping from gratitude to resentment, envy, bitterness or despair...forgetting that creative power is always our secret weapon.

It's precisely at moments like these that we are most negatively vulnerable and must guard our thoughts carefully. Since our thinking creates the nature of the events and circumstances in our lives, resentment, envy, bitterness or despair will produce their harvest just as readily as a more positive reaction.

A grateful attitude, however, will leave us open to the insights found in each challenge we face and open to learning something important about ourselves, because *there is a lesson of value in each apparent adversity.*

Gratefully label everything "good," then work to prove your label was right!

I CHOOSE TO SEE MY CRISIS AS AN OPPORTUNITY!

…but here we go again.

No matter who we are, it's hard to avoid experiencing a crisis of some kind at some time in our lives.

At those moments, the tendency to become despondent, nervous or desperate is not uncommon and can often seem overwhelming.

These are the times, however, when our thinking needs to be at its very clearest for, whether we realize it or not, by the clarity of our thought, we are actually determining the *effect* each particular crisis will have on us. Clear thinking is a requirement.

By keeping our own thoughts cheerful, optimistic and confidently expectant, we set a good example for others involved, often eliminating the potential for anxiety or hysteria that might result.

At the same time, with a positive, expectant and receptive attitude, we are creating within ourselves an atmosphere that draws the answers to us, that can bring us the solutions and opportunities we need to handle the situation.

Understand that each crisis in life contains an *opportunity,* and *look for it*!

I CHOOSE TO LOOK FORWARD NOT BACKWARDS!

…but it seems like I am stuck in the past.

As we move on through life, there is a tendency to get bogged down with accumulated feelings of failure, missed opportunities, frustration and guilt.

Any of these can easily result in a sense of futility that can slowly seep into all aspects of our being.

We find ourselves looking back...wishing we could try it again...wishing we had another chance...wishing we had known then what we know now. The fact is, of course, that there's no way it can be done. We can't go back.

We did what we did when we did it because that was the way we perceived things at that place in time. Those actions represented our level of awareness at those particular moments, nothing more and nothing less.

Presumably we could do better with our present level of understanding today than we did then. But yesterday is gone, and the question becomes what are we going to do right now?

If we feel we've gained additional insights that better equip us to deal with life, why waste time bemoaning the past when we have a golden opportunity to apply them today? *No matter what has happened before, it is never too late to make a fresh beginning, a new start*!

It is never too late to forgive ourselves for our past shortcomings and restore that feeling of excitement to our lives by living them with an attitude of *positive expectancy*! Then was then – and *now is now*. Make the most of it!

I CHOOSE TO LEARN FROM MY MISTAKES!

...but I'm afraid I'll look stupid.

Too many good ideas never get much further than the mind of the person thinking them because they're afraid of making mistakes.

We are often so concerned about what people will think of us if we fail that we hold back from doing anything that involves the risk of failure.

Success at any venture requires *vision, conviction* and *action*. We must take whatever action seems appropriate and keep our vision focused on the belief that, in the long run, nothing can keep us from our goal.

If things do appear to go wrong at times, don't despair or run away embarrassed. Remember that we all make mistakes. There is no shame in it. Too often, it's merely a matter of not having our action properly coordinated with our vision and conviction.

Learn from your mistakes! Use the lessons wisely. They are pointing out something important that needs to be adjusted.

Above all, never let any mistake turn you away from your ultimate objective. The people laughing or pointing a finger when you stumble will be the same ones shaking your hand when you've succeeded!

I CHOOSE TO CALL THE SHOTS AND FIND THE PERFECT SOLUTION!

…but I really just want to throw my hands in the air and give up.

Even the best of us have our worst moments – times when nothing appears to be going right, and we seem to be at a dead end. What do we do then?

What we have to do is decide on the response we will make. We can give up in despair, or we can decide to do something constructive about it.

Which choice it will be depends on how clearly we understand the fact that we are in full control of our responses. *We* call the shots, and *we* can create a successful ending for this situation just as easily as for any other kind.

Those that do will turn away from their momentary distress and tell themselves, "There is an ultimate source of all knowledge, and I intend to use it right now. I intend to find the perfect solution to this challenge, because I know there *is* one."

Each of us, whether we realize it or not, has the capability of doing just that. This *unlimited creative power has been given equally to us all.* When positively and productively directed by the strength of our belief, it enables us to emerge triumphant over every obstacle in our lives!

I CHOOSE TO REGROUP, KNOWING IT'S A PRELUDE FOR SUCCESS!

…but it all just seems so hopeless.

It can be one of the most important things any of us will ever do.

Regrouping is a process each of us can carry out after a disappointment, frustration or defeat. It is the time when we are confronted with the results of whatever has not gone well, and we are appraising the situation.

What will it be? Even if the event has been painful – no matter what our sense of rejection, despair or failure – will we have the courage and honesty to carefully examine the clues to what went wrong which will enable us to eventually triumph?

There is no disgrace in failing. When seen through the eyes of the positive thinker, it becomes merely a matter of having temporarily missed the mark, a *prelude* for inevitable success. History is one story after another of targets that were initially missed by those who learned from their mistakes and subsequently overcame them.

For the person dedicated to accomplishing a particular goal, a constructive approach to regrouping is *mandatory*, because inherent in every failure is the key to ultimate victory.

Never settle for less!

I CHOOSE
TO TAKE
A CHANCE!

…but I'm too old and I just don't have the guts.

How many things do we avoid doing, and how many opportunities for creative expression do we pass up because we're afraid?

How many of us nourish a secret desire to sing, act, play an instrument, build something or go back to school? And yet, we're hesitant to pursue these desires because of *fear*... the fear that we'd fail, wouldn't be good enough, or be laughed at by others.

Being laughed at by someone, somewhere, at sometime is probably impossible to avoid, no matter who we are. Because of this inevitability, we would be well advised to work our way through that as soon as possible.

When we're afraid we'll fail, or that we can't pull something off, remember that we are dealing primarily with a matter of confidence, since science has clearly shown we all are capable of accomplishing far more than we are presently doing because we are actually only using a small part of our brain.

Life belongs to the bold, those who are willing to be laughed at, if that's what it takes, but who refuse to view things exclusively from a spectator's seat.

Start today to do what you've always wanted. Take that first step, whatever it may be. Stretch yourself! Take a chance! You'll be surprised at what you can do!

I CHOOSE NO-LIMIT THINKING!

…but there's no way to get there from here.

Amazing things would happen if we all indulged in a week of *no-limit* thinking.

One week when we gave ourselves full permission to let our imaginations soar, unrestricted.

One week of not agonizing over *how* we'd accomplish what we desired but, instead, just focused on the fact that it *could* be done.

This one-week could change our entire approach to life!

You see, nothing can dampen the spirit like *limited* thinking. Why? Because it is foreign to our true nature; it goes completely against the grain.

We each have been given the use of a creative power without limitation in its ability to produce. It can manifest *any* idea presented to it with total, unwavering belief. *Any idea*!

The significant accomplishments of mankind have all been made by those who practiced *no-limit-thinking*... by those who paid no attention to what others said couldn't be done and, instead, opened their minds to the fact that there are *unlimited possibilities* available at any time *if* we have the *courage* to claim them for ourselves.

Add life to your years. Bring back the excitement of knowingly creating your own destiny. Take off the brakes of limited thinking, and let yourself go. Discover that there are no limits other than the ones we impose on ourselves!

I CHOOSE TO MOVE FORWARD!

…but I feel really defeated.

Failure and defeat may appear to be no more than different words that mean the same thing, but they are not.

Failure is something we've all experienced but, if handled properly, it becomes just one more step forward towards the ultimate achievement of our goals, even though it may have been a painful experience at the time.

Defeat is a matter that indicates an entirely different state of mind. While failure is only a *temporary event* along the road leading to eventual success, defeat means a person believes they've already come to the end of the road.

Defeat means that, instead of looking on failure as a prelude to triumph, a sometimes-necessary part of the process, we have given up. In the frustration of not being able to immediately achieve our goal, we have made a decision to quit. In cutting off any further pursuit of our objective, we have surrendered to the belief that it can't be done – at least by us.

In either case, the power of *belief* would have made it so. Turn your failures into success and never be defeated!

I CHOOSE TO GIVE LOVE!

…but I have no love to give.

Rejection of one kind or another is something many of us fear more than any other, and it can be a bitter pill to swallow, especially when it seems undeserved.

To *feel* loved is one of our greatest needs. To *express* love is another, and when either is lacking in our lives, look out! It can spell trouble with a capital T.

People who feel rejected often react by cutting off the flow of their love to others and become, instead, defiant or sullen or moody. This only creates more turmoil.

Why swallow that bitter pill at all? Why let anyone else's response, or lack of it, make us sad, bitter or hostile?

What is needed at these crucial times is not an attitude of belligerent resistance, but one of *greater understanding*. Finding the other person's point of view can frequently help us see that rejection was not their intent at all. And even if it was, there is nothing to be gained and much to be lost if we respond by withdrawing into our protective shells.

Expressing love is an absolute essential for maintaining a healthy state of well-being. If we focus on *giving* love, the *getting* will take care of itself, and there'll be no time for concern about rejection, imagined or otherwise!

I CHOOSE TO ACCEPT YOU AND ME WITHOUT JUDGMENT!

…but judging others is something that I've always done.

Is there anyone more highly regarded than the person who has mastered the art of making others feel good about themselves?

The person who habitually treats others with respect, courtesy, consideration and kindness is always at a premium and will be sought out by those who enjoy being with someone who practices the golden rule of successful relationships.

And is it really so hard to do? Is it so difficult to relate to others without feeling superior, defensive, hostile, unworthy or inadequate?

Is it so hard to see that we are all on the same path of understanding together, with some just a little further along and others a little behind?

Is it so difficult to accept ourselves, along with others, as being right where we are without feeling the need to pass judgment? Without trying to make ourselves feel more important by making someone else feel less so?

There is *something* within each of us that is the *same*, no matter what our surface differences may be. Understand that, deep down, this is the part of us that wants to be expressed and recognized. Then do your best to respond to others at that point. It will work wonders for all concerned!

I CHOOSE TO FEED MYSELF HEALTHY FOODS AND THOUGHTS!

...but do good thoughts really make a difference?

Many of us are far more concerned about what we feed our bodies than what we feed our minds. Even if we would never eat the so-called junk foods that glut the market today, we feed ourselves junk thoughts without even a raised eyebrow.

Junk *thoughts*, like junk *foods*, are unhealthy. They have no constructive value whatsoever.

Never forget that the conditions in our lives are dictated by the ideas in our minds.

What kind of a mental diet are you currently on? Does it contain thoughts that you want to see take place in your life? Are there ideas of prosperity? Health? Happiness? Peace? Love? Harmony?

In the final analysis, *we each experience what we give our energy and attention to* – those thoughts that we allow to become our deepest-held beliefs, our convictions. Either fill your mind with healthy ideas, or you'll find their opposite taking over and appearing as your experiences.

You deserve the best. Eat good food for a healthy body; think good thoughts for a healthy life!

I CHOOSE TO LISTEN!

…but I don't understand why listening is so important.

One of the greatest of all the arts, and perhaps the finest, is the art of *listening*. It is also one of the least practiced.

How often do we yearn for someone who will just *listen* to us? Not give advice, not relate what we are saying to their experiences, but just listen?

The desire to be thought important is something within us all, and we all *are* important. There are few things that can make us feel any better about ourselves than to have an interested, attentive listener, one who will put aside their personal needs for expressing feelings or receiving recognition and listen only to us.

The good listener gives us an opportunity to release many thoughts and feelings that need venting, the kind that can easily produce all kinds of difficulties when they are allowed to fester within.

The good listener, perhaps even more importantly, allows us to often hear ourselves say the very things that provide the key to resolving the difficulties we ourselves are confronted with.

We *all* need listeners. Why not take time each day to practice the art of being a good listener? You will be pleasantly surprised by what it can do for *both* of you.

I CHOOSE TO DEVELOP THE PRAISE HABIT!

...but who has time for that?

What are the sweetest words we can hear? They are words of praise. None of us can get too much. Most don't get enough.

By *genuinely* and *sincerely* praising people, we are often making a significant contribution to their positive feelings about themselves. Through our eyes, they come to see themselves more lovingly and kindly. Their self-image is enhanced, and they then can function at a new level of self-awareness.

The art of praise is one we would all do well to cultivate. We should make it a point to take the time at home, on the job and in public, to express our appreciation for the good qualities and the good work of those we come in contact with. It should become an enduring habit we never give up, since we need never fear offending anyone with sincere admiration and gratitude.

By looking for the good in others and praising it, we are doing ourselves a service too, as we tend to experience in our lives what we are giving our energy and attention to.

Many of us have been helped by someone who encouraged us with a word of praise at the right time. Make it a regular habit and enjoy the dividends!

I CHOOSE
TO LOVE MYSELF
AND
NOURISH OTHERS!

…but I just feel so ordinary.

Is it possible to die from a lack of love? Researchers are increasingly confirming that it is. Some say it may well be the leading cause of all death and illness, if the truth were known.

Of course, the death certificates and hospital reports may indicate other reasons, but the underlying fact could be that the individual either lost, or never developed, an ability to love and be loved. Thus, the old concept of love or perish would appear to be receiving even further validation with each study.

Enlightened men and women down through the ages have given us much wisdom to live by, and it all points to love as a *human essential*. It includes the unparalleled area of *self-love*, being able to see ourselves through the eyes of love and lovingly *accepting* ourselves.

This is the love that recognizes our complete worthiness to experience the very best that life has to offer. This is the kind that enables us to nourish others with love because we have nourished *ourselves* first.

Give yourself the best present possible, the gift of self-love. Then, share it with others!

I CHOOSE TO DO MY JOB WELL, WHILE PREPARING FOR THE NEXT STEP!

…but I hate my job.

Many people wind up working at jobs that are far different from the ones they once dreamed of doing, and they resent every minute of it. People, who work at what they always planned to do, and genuinely enjoy it, are fortunate. For them, their daily work is a new adventure, something they eagerly look forward to doing.

Suppose, though, you're one of those who aren't happy in the job you have. Are you doomed to a life of drudgery and unhappiness in your work? Not necessarily.

The first step towards getting satisfaction from any job is to do it well. It's also the first step towards a promotion. If conditions are such that you're not doing the thing you'd ideally like, then do what you're doing in an *ideal* manner. Give it your best. Concentrate your efforts on what you're doing at the moment, and don't waste time looking at the place you'd hoped to be or ahead to where you wish you were.

Be *grateful* for the job you have at the moment and find things you like about it. There's *always something* to be thankful for.

Set goals for yourself. While doing your best at your present job, prepare for what you plan to be doing by gaining whatever education or experience you'll need to move on out when the time is right.

Finally, let your positive attitude be the result of knowing that you are *never* limited by anything, at anytime, unless *you* impose those limits by your own thinking!

I CHOOSE TO UNITE WITH MY GOOD!

...but I'm still alone.

Loneliness is a disease. That's the bad news. The good news is that there *is* a cure!

People who draw to themselves those who betray or disappoint them can easily come to believe this is just the way things are in the world, fencing themselves off from others to the point that life becomes a lonely existence. And it *is* lonely *if* we buy into the belief that we are ever separated from the *ultimate source* of our good.

This is never the case. No matter how much it may seem so, the connection itself is always there!

Life never gives us anything we have not first generally accepted at some level for ourselves. Thus, if people feel the only viable defense against further hurt is to withdraw, they are only compounding their self-inflicted misery.

The ensuing loneliness is the result of an error in their thinking, a belief that something outside themselves is controlling their lives. This, however, is an illusion. *All control comes from within.* We are *each* in our own driver's seat at all times. We each attract or push away with our thoughts.

We experience the results of our most deeply held beliefs about ourselves and, by so doing, have the opportunity of seeing our beliefs for what they are.

If we don't like those results, let's change our beliefs. We are only shut off from others if *we* do the shutting. Release the lonely past, accept personal responsibility and start building a happier future right now!

I CHOOSE TO TREAT OTHERS AS I WANT TO BE TREATED!

…but anger is natural.

Anger is something we all have to deal with at times, but *how* do we deal with it?

Are the people who vent their anger better off than those who don't, as has been popularly supposed?

According to new evidence, *they are not.* Those who give their explosive emotions free reign have been found to be more likely to have heart attacks and related illnesses.

Shooting from the hip, so to speak, was once promoted on the theory it is better to get it out than keep it in. It's been found, however, that to do so as a way of life puts one under damaging emotional and physical stress that could be either reduced or eliminated completely with a more moderate, understanding approach.

Furthermore, there is no telling how much additional irritation may be caused by the damaged personal relationships resulting from just venting one's feelings of anger whenever there's an opportunity.

When all is said and done, the ultimate solution to successfully dealing with this kind of anger is found in the old adage of *doing unto others, as you would have them do unto you.* Turn your anger into something that shows you at your best!

I CHOOSE TO REMAIN POSITIVELY EXPECTANT!

...but this is my health I'm talking about.

It's hard to believe that the difference between life and death can often hinge on nothing more than a *thought*, but the evidence keeps mounting that this is true.

Doctors, psychologists, ministers and health care workers see it every day, and gradually others are becoming more aware of the dramatic effects *attitudes* can have on one's well being.

Even so, it's often difficult convincing people that they, themselves, can be their own worst enemy. It's surprisingly easy for most of us to become overwhelmed with anxiety at certain times and, depending on the situation, find ourselves giving in to depression, despair or even hopelessness.

None of these are conducive to good health or to effectively resolving the problem. Hopelessness, in fact, can often prove fatal. University experiments with rats in a controlled situation showed that when confronted with what seemed like a hopeless situation, their bodily functions not only slowed down, but eventually stopped. Similar studies with human beings indicate that the same thing takes place to a greater or lesser degree as they give in to feelings of hopelessness.

Just as thoughts can *kill*, however, they can also *heal* and keep the body operating in harmony and health!

I CHOOSE A "HAVE" CONSCIOUSNESS!

…but I've been poor for such a long time.

There is a difference between being broke and being poor and it's a *big* one.

We can all be broke at different times in our lives, but it doesn't mean it's anything more than just a stop along the road.

On the other hand, being poor is something else entirely. And it all boils down to a matter of *consciousness* – the sum total of our thoughts.

Ours is either a *have* or a *have-not* consciousness regarding money. People with a *have* consciousness may be temporarily broke, but won't stay that way for long. Most certainly, they will never be poor. They will always find a way to acquire more money from somewhere.

Those with a *have-not* consciousness will produce an entirely different set of conditions. Poverty will find its way to them, and they will most often wind up on the losing end of things as far as money is concerned.

Is it due to lucky breaks or fate? No, it isn't. Our financial abundance, or lack, is basically determined by our belief. A *have-not* consciousness comes from the belief that we are *separated* from the source of our good, while the *have* consciousness is exactly the opposite. Recognize the difference and make the most of it!

I CHOOSE TO ACCEPT SUCCESS AS POSSIBLE FOR ME!

...but I sure don't feel like a success.

Success is something that intrigues just about everybody. It's something that most of us feel we could always use more of. Success in love, success in business, success in dealing with others, success in doing what we'd like, success in being the kind of person we want to be.

Usually, the *aware* person who is successful at one thing will also be successful at others, because the formula for success is the same for all. *Success is a way of thinking.* It all begins in the mind. To be successful, we must first *see* ourselves as being successful...we must *accept* ourselves as being *worthy* of success...*entitled* to success by the very nature of our being. *We must know we were never created to be anything less and prepare accordingly.*

Success, then, becomes a matter of first knowing this truth about ourselves...then, directing our thoughts and efforts in an expectant manner!

Take a good, hard look at yourself today. If you're not successful in all areas of your life, who's kidding who? Who's denying their true identity? Their true capabilities?

Who's pretending to be somebody they're not? Who's settling for less than they're entitled to? Who's yearning for something they've *already* got?

Declare your freedom from doubt and fear and make room for the success that is rightfully yours!

I CHOOSE TO HONOR MY CREATIVE POWER!

...but how do I tap into it?

The self-reliant person is the one to watch. This person has recognized his creative power and uses it constructively. This is the person who never feels a victim of circumstances or needs to stand in anybody's shadow.

This is the person who will thrill to the feeling of power that comes to those who trust their own judgment, keep their own counsel, and expectantly look to the one unlimited, ultimate, universal source for everything necessary to fulfill any worthwhile purpose. This is the person who will fearlessly face all challenges, convinced that any apparent failure is only an opportunity in disguise.

The self-reliant person will never fall by the roadside of life in despair. Nor will destructive self-doubts and fears plague them. This person will, instead, walk courageously forward, never faltering in the belief that the path ahead will ultimately lead to their goal.

The self-reliant person will make the most of each moment but will have an eye for making the future even better with vision undimmed by the shortsightedness of others.

The self-reliant person will not look to others as a source of supply or power. Without question, this person will commit to accomplishing any desire for greater good, knowing that the act of such commitment reflects the quality of belief necessary for accomplishment!

I CHOOSE TO FOLLOW THROUGH WITH MY DESIRES!

…but I've tried that before and failed.

The creative power within is awesome in its ability to achieve! Those who can properly *focus* this power on a particular goal will inevitably find themselves experiencing success. One of the ironies of life is that the things we often only dream of accomplishing are actually right within our grasp, and we simply don't realize it.

We obviously have been created with not only desires, but with the capacity for turning them into realities. There is a great difference, however, between being *able* to do what we want and actually *doing* it. Those whose initial *desires* seem the strongest can often mislead us into assuming they will automatically reach their destination. Unfortunately, there is nothing automatic about it.

To achieve success at anything, it's necessary to *keep* our thought energy at a consistently high level. This calls for carefully selecting a goal in the first place and making it something you can see taking place. You then must know, without question, that you're dealing with an inner power that is *without limit* in its capacity to draw to you everything that will ultimately turn your pursuit into victory.

Finally, it takes a positive *follow-through* with *everything* you think, say and do...a follow-through that reflects your *conviction and never wavers*!

I CHOOSE DISCIPLINED BELIEF TO REACH MY GOALS!

...but I'm not a disciplined person.

There are few words that cause many of us to recoil more than *discipline*. Our reaction often comes from childhood when discipline meant punishment of one kind or another.

As an adult, however, discipline should be a sought-after prize because it implies control over life's energies and enthusiasms. Discipline often represents the difference between success and failure.

The person able to keep his thinking centered on a particular objective stands a far greater chance of accomplishment than the one who can't keep their goals in focus.

The ability to discipline one's appetites can have far-reaching rewards in physical and emotional wellness. Being in conscious control enables a person to be truly flexible when the occasion calls for it, rather than locked into a series of reflex actions.

There is great joy in accomplishment, and the disciplined person will always triumph over the deadening paralysis of laziness. They will always triumph over those who give up in defeat.

Disciplined people, who know they are dealing with an inner power which never says no, will *persevere* in spite of those who say they can't make it. Their disciplined belief will enable them to continue even after all reasonable hope has vanished, and they will eventually snatch ultimate victory from the jaws of defeat. Make disciplined thinking your constant companion and experience the rewards!

I CHOOSE TO LOOK FOR CAUSES AND SOLUTIONS!

...but bad things just happen to me.

Who is your worst enemy? *You are*! In fact, you are your *only* enemy.

None of us is ever ultimately defeated by anyone or anything outside ourselves. It all has to start with a thought in mind first.

If you find things in your life that are unpleasant; if you find opportunities seemingly at a dead end; if you find yourself apparently locked into hateful, angry or resentful relationships, stop looking for outside causes because there aren't any.

Painful as it may be to face, these kinds of conditions will continue to plague us until there has been a *change* in the thought patterns that attracted them in the first place – a release of unworthy, inadequate or inferior beliefs.

There is *always* a cause, *always* a reason. But, there is also *always* a solution.

Look for the cause with the complete expectation that you'll find it. You'll be amazed at what you discover. Once revealed, make whatever changes are called for. *Remember that while your thinking created the problem, it can resolve it, too.*

Self-appreciation, love and acceptance are the keys. Instead of being your own worst enemy, become your own best friend!

I CHOOSE TO BE GRATEFUL FOR EACH EXPERIENCE!

...but what will that do for me?

Appreciation is only an attitude, but what a difference it can make.

People who are genuinely thankful for everything they have in their lives, whether called good or bad by others, have gone a long way towards truly tapping into one of the great secrets of the universe.

Each experience can teach us something of value, something each of us needs to know or be reminded of.

By gratefully accepting this for a fact and not resisting it, our opportunities for growth increase enormously. And the greater our understanding, the more clearly we see that life is good, that it is meant to be enjoyed, that we have every reason to be grateful 100% of the time.

Appreciation is the attitude we should never be without!

I CHOOSE TO CREATE THE RIGHT OPPORTUNITY AT ALL TIMES!

…but I'm never in the right place at the right time.

Many of us yearn for the sweet fruits of success, but many are frustrated by our apparent inability to reach them and, feeling hopeless, we eventually accept the notion that we never really had a chance.

The plain truth, however, is *many of us don't really know what we're doing*! Like a five-year-old at the controls of a jet airplane, we lack the knowledge to get ourselves properly launched.

When speaking of achieving success in the theatre, Sir Laurence Olivier said, "You must first have the humility to prepare and then the confidence to pull it off."

Success at whatever endeavor we may choose is a potential any of us might realize, but in order to make that potential a reality, it does take that combination.

In spite of the labor that is often involved, the preparatory work is often the least of our problems. The real challenge comes in confidently putting what we have learned into its proper niche so we have the necessary outlet to express ourselves successfully.

This requires *conviction*, a conviction that – no matter what the competition, no matter what the economic climate of the day – we have, within our thinking, the ability to create the right opportunity at all times.

Those who know there is such a power within themselves, and who believingly use it, will *always* have the confidence to pull it off, no matter what they choose!

I CHOOSE TO
MAKE THE MOST
OF MY POTENTIAL
IN ALL AREAS
OF MY LIFE
BY TRUSTNG,
RELYING ON
AND USING THE
CREATIVE POWER
WITHIN ME
AT ALL TIMES!

About the author

Don McArt has been a successful college bandleader, radio personality, Broadway and Hollywood actor/director, television writer/producer, Las Vegas comedian, metaphysical speaker and author...BUT it hasn't always been easy!

Stricken with a brain tumor at an early age, he overcame serious illness, in spite of dire predictions – and, in the process, became fascinated with the inner workings of the mind and what effect it has on both one's physical well-being and, indeed, one's ultimate chance of achieving any goal.

Eventually he discovered, to his own satisfaction, that a strong, unyielding belief in each individual's power of mind seemed to be the common denominator behind virtually all significant achievements, regardless of the religious, economic, ethnic, intellectual or educational backgrounds of those involved.

He also found that many enlightened people before him, in their own words, had declared this to be the way they believed life works.

Determined to reduce this creative principle to its bare essence, free of any doctrine and dogma, Mr. McArt has written his book with the hope that it will give insight and courage to all those who want to take better control of their lives and fulfill their particular dreams.